THE OFFICIAL
ENGLAND
ANNUAL 2013

Written by Jon Culley

Designed by Jane Massey

A Grange Publication

© 2012. Published by Grange Communications Ltd., Edinburgh, under licence from The Football Association Ltd. Printed in the EU.

Every effort has been made to ensure the accuracy of information within this publication but the publishers cannot be held responsible for any errors or omissions. Views expressed are those of the author and do not necessarily represent those of the publishers or The Football Association. All rights reserved. Content correct as of September 2012

Photography© Action Images

© The Football Association Ltd 2012. The FA Crest and FA England Crest are official trademarks of The Football Association Ltd and are the subject of extensive trademark registrations worldwide

ISBN: 978-1-908925-04-6

£7.99

CONTENTS

England manager Roy Hodgson arrived at the FA with an impressive CV when he was appointed as Fabio Capello's successor.

The Making of Roy
Roy Hodgson in profile

His record included eight championships in three countries, as well as three national cups, and he twice took teams to the Final of the UEFA Cup. Fluent in five languages and comfortable in four others, with a sophisticated taste in literature and music, Hodgson arrived as the ultimate cosmopolitan football man.

To reach that point, however, he had come on a very long journey spanning 36 years in management. Hodgson, from a working class background in Croydon, had a modest playing career in non-League football. He turned to coaching at an early age. He was only 23 when he gained his full badge.

His first management position was as an assistant at Maidstone United to Bob Houghton, an old schoolmate who was to become a significant figure in helping Hodgson establish himself.

Houghton's career took him to Sweden, where he coached Malmo to two championships in a row in the early 1970s. He recommended Hodgson to FC Halmstad. They were favourites for relegation in 1976 but Hodgson transformed their fortunes so dramatically they were Swedish champions in his first season and retained the title the following year.

After a brief stint back in England, working at Bristol City, Hodgson returned to Sweden, ultimately taking his mentor Houghton's former position at Malmo. Again he was spectacularly successful, winning five titles in a row.

Malmo offered him a job for life but Hodgson was ambitious. He moved to Switzerland, where he guided Neuchatel Xamax to notable victories over Celtic and Real Madrid in Europe before being appointed as coach of the Swiss national side.

Switzerland had never been a major force in international football. Yet under Hodgson's guidance, they reached the World Cup Finals in 1994 – for the first time since 1966 – and finished second in their group, before losing to Spain in the round of 16.

The Swiss team qualified easily for Euro '96 but Hodgson passed up the chance to lead them in a tournament in his home country, instead accepting his biggest club role to that point, with Internazionale in Italy.

In a country notorious for its high turnover of coaches, Hodgson remained at Inter for a season and half and enjoyed some success. He took over during the 1995-96 season with Inter struggling, yet qualified for the UEFA Cup, in which his team reached the Final, losing to Schalke 0-4 on penalties.

The next decade saw Hodgson manage club sides in five countries as well as two international teams, the United Arab Emirates and Finland. He had more success – he won the Superliga in Denmark with FC Copenhagen.

He took Blackburn Rovers into the UEFA Cup in his first season but paid the price when they dropped to the bottom of the table the following year. A spell in charge of Liverpool ended after only 31 games in charge.

In between, he enhanced his reputation with a successful stint as Fulham boss. Taking over in 2007, Hodgson saved the London club from relegation, guided them to a highest-ever seventh place in 2008-09 and reached the Final of the UEFA Europa League the following year, the first major European Final in the club's 130-year history. Fulham lost 2-1 to Atletico Madrid in the Final, but Hodgson had already been voted Manager of the Year by his fellow bosses by a record margin.

When the call came to become England boss, Hodgson was in charge at West Bromwich Albion, where he endeared himself to fans by leading them to their highest finishing League position in 30 years in 2010-11 and doing the 'double' over arch Black Country rivals Wolves in 2011-12, including a 5-1 win at Molineux.

DID YOU KNOW?

In the 1970s, Roy Hodgson was a PE teacher at Alleyn's School in Dulwich, South London.

THEIR FINEST HOURS

The story of England's managers told through their best results...

SIR WALTER WINTERBOTTOM (1946-62)

Italy 0 England 4
May 16, 1948; Turin; friendly

WINTERBOTTOM'S RECORD

P 139 W 78 D 33 L 28

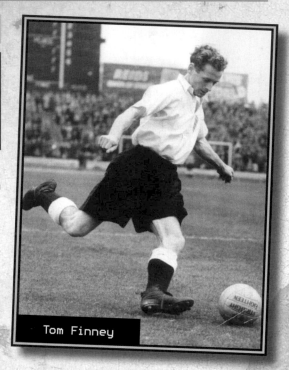

Tom Finney

Winterbottom took England to four World Cup Finals, reaching the last eight twice, yet was also at the helm when England suffered their first-ever home defeat to continental opposition, losing 6-3 to Hungary in 1953. The result shattered England's tactical conventions, the blow compounded when they lost 7-1 in a return match in Budapest.

Yet in May, 1948 Winterbottom is hailed as a master tactician – at least in Italy – after England humiliate an Italian side then regarded as the best in Europe, on their own turf. In a superb display of counter-attacking, goals from Stan Mortensen, Tommy Lawton and Tom Finney (two) give England a 4-0 win.

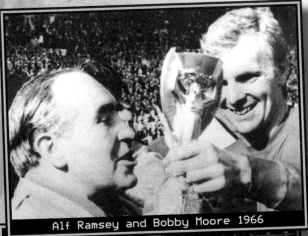

Alf Ramsey and Bobby Moore 1966

1966 World Cup

SIR ALF RAMSEY (1963-74)

England 4 West Germany 2
July 30, 1966; Wembley; World Cup Final

RAMSEY'S RECORD

P 113 W 69 D 27 L 17

Ramsey always believed he would win the World Cup on home soil and his conviction was borne out in a thrilling 1966 Final that remains the greatest moment in England's history.

Helmut Haller (12 minutes) puts the Germans in front, Geoff Hurst (18 mins) equalises and Martin Peters (78 mins) gives England the lead only for Wolfgang Weber to square the scores again with a minute left. Extra time brings controversy as Hurst's second goal stands despite uncertainty over whether the ball crossed the line, but the argument becomes academic as Hurst scores again. It is so close to the end that, with some England fans already on the pitch to celebrate victory, commentator Kenneth Wolstenholme is prompted to deliver his immortal line: "They think it's all over..." pausing just long enough for Hurst's shot to slam into the German net before adding "...it is now. It's four."

JOE MERCER (1974)

Yugoslavia 2 England 2
June 5, 1974; Belgrade; friendly

MERCER'S RECORD

P 7 W 3 D 3 L 1

Malcolm Macdonald   Colin Bell
Don Revie

Genial Joe Mercer's brief stint as caretaker manager required him unexpectedly to reveal diplomatic skills in the build-up to his final match in charge. This followed a bizarre incident at Belgrade Airport in which police took exception to some England players larking about in the baggage hall and arrested Kevin Keegan. The Liverpool forward was roughed up and detained for more than an hour by his captors, who made a number of allegations against him, all of which were dropped after Mercer joined other officials in persuading police to let him go.

In the match, Mick Channon gives England an early lead, Yugoslavia score twice but Keegan, ironically, has the last laugh, scoring a 75th-minute equaliser.

DON REVIE (1974-77)

England 2 West Germany 0
March 12, 1975; Wembley; friendly

REVIE'S RECORD

P 29 W 14 D 8 L 7

Revie's reign was to end in acrimony as the former Leeds manager quit to accept a lucrative job in the Middle East, having failed to qualify for the 1976 European Championship. Yet his third match in charge – the 100th international at Wembley – dealt the Germans a convincing defeat, their first since winning the 1974 World Cup.

Revie makes veteran Alan Ball skipper and teams him with Colin Bell and the brilliantly talented Alan Hudson, who produce a superb performance capped by a deflected opening goal by Bell and a first for England by the Newcastle striker Malcolm Macdonald.

Revie stuck with the same midfield against Cyprus in a European Championship qualifier the following month, when Macdonald scored all five goals. Yet he never picked Hudson again and in time dispensed with both Ball and Macdonald.

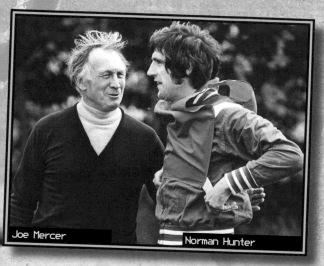
Joe Mercer   Norman Hunter

RON GREENWOOD (1977-82)

England 3 France 1
June 16, 1982; Bilbao; World Cup

GREENWOOD'S RECORD

P 40 W 26 D 8 L 6

Greenwood was unable to pick up the pieces quickly enough for England to qualify for the 1978 World Cup and his side were early casualties in the 1980 European Championship Finals but the avuncular former West Ham boss steered England into the 1982 World Cup Finals, where they opened with a stunning win over France.

Bryan Robson scores after just 27 seconds – at that time the fastest goal in the history of the tournament - and though France equalise, Robson heads a second after half-time and Paul Mariner clinches victory.

England went on to beat Czechoslovakia and Kuwait in the opening phase and were unlucky to be eliminated undefeated after goalless draws against West Germany and Spain in a second group phase.

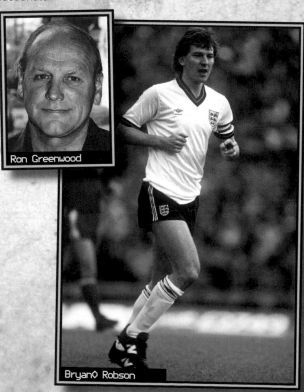
Ron Greenwood   Bryan Robson

SIR BOBBY ROBSON (1982-90)

West Germany 1 England 1
July 4, 1990; Turin; World Cup semi-final;
West Germany win 4-3 on penalties
___ ___ ___
ROBSON'S RECORD
P 95 W 47 D 30 L 18

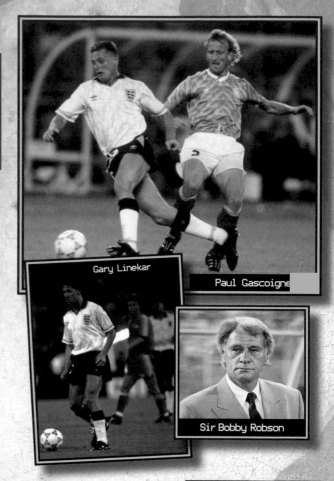

Gary Linekar

Paul Gascoigne

Robson rode several peaks and troughs as England manager, appearing more than once to be on the verge of losing the job. But he hung on and was unlucky not to become the second manager to lead England to a World Cup Final after an epic Italia '90 semi-final against West Germany.

In a game marked by a superb performance by Paul Gascoigne – memorable for more than the tears he shed when a yellow card meant he would miss the Final – a freakish deflection off Paul Parker from an Andreas Brehme shot gives the Germans a 59th-minute lead. But Gary Lineker hits a terrific left-foot shot to equalise 10 minutes from time. In extra time both sides hit the post but it comes down to penalties and broken hearts as Stuart Pearce and Chris Waddle miss theirs and West Germany go through.

Sir Bobby Robson

Graham Taylor (1990-93)

England 2 France 0
Feb 19, 1992; Wembley; friendly
___ ___ ___
TAYLOR'S RECORD
P 38 W 18 D 13 L 7

Taylor's tenure is remembered for his fractious relationship with striker and captain, Gary Lineker, for the farcical failure of the 1994 World Cup qualifying campaign and for the vicious treatment dished out by the press after England's 1992 European Championship ended with defeat by Sweden. Yet he served England well in a prestige friendly against France early in the same year by giving a debut to 21-year-old Alan Shearer, then with Southampton.

He is rewarded with a Shearer goal and arguably the best performance of his time in charge to end a 19-match unbeaten run by the French. Lineker, left on the bench after announcing he would retire in the summer, comes off the bench to add the second.

Alan Shearer

Graham Taylor

Gary Linekar and Alan Shearer

Terry Venables (1994-96)

Netherlands 1 England 4
June 18, 1996; Wembley;
European Championships

VENABLE'S RECORD

P **24** W **11** D **14** L **1**

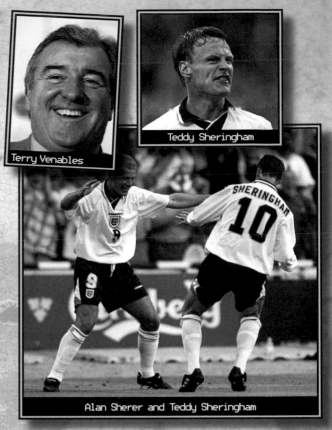

Terry Venables

Teddy Sheringham

Alan Sherer and Teddy Sheringham

A long media campaign to persuade The FA to install Venables as manager succeeded in 1994 and although his period in charge lasted only two years before his complicated business life again became a distraction it was long enough to include one of England's finest tournament performances since the 1966 World Cup.

Encouraged to express their attacking instincts, England gain a slightly fortunate half-time lead through an Alan Shearer penalty but take the Dutch apart in the second half, scoring three times in the first 17 minutes. The star is Teddy Sheringham, who scores two goals and caps a brilliant move involving Paul Gascoigne and Steve McManaman by cleverly teeing up Shearer for his second.

Lasting glory eluded Venables, however, when England lost to Germany (again) in a penalty shoot-out (again) in the semi-finals.

Glenn Hoddle (1996-98)

Argentina 2 England 2
June 30, 1998; St Etienne; World Cup;
Argentina won 4-3 on penalties

HODDLE'S RECORD

P **28** W **17** D **6** L **5**

Michael Owen

Glenn Hoddle

G lenn Hoddle might have become one of England's great managers had he not discussed some controversial beliefs in an interview with The Times. The furore that followed ended with Prime Minister Tony Blair calling for his dismissal on daytime television. In any case, Hoddle appeared no less cursed by penalties than his predecessors after a captivating display in this second-round match at France '98.

England trail after five minutes to a Gabriel Batistuta penalty but are level after 10 when Alan Shearer scores from the spot. Then 18-year-old Michael Owen puts them ahead, sprinting past two defenders and smashing the ball home. However, Javier Zanetti equalises for Argentina before half-time. England lose David Beckham to a red card in the first minute of the second half but fight on and have a Sol Campbell header dubiously disallowed. After a goalless extra time, the result is settled by a penalty shoot-out, which goes 4-3 in Argentina's favour after Paul Ince and David Batty miss for England.

Kevin Keegan (1999-2000)

England 1 Germany 0

June 17, 2000; Charleroi, Belgium;
European Championship

KEEGAN'S RECORD

P **18** W **7** D **7** L **4**

Kevin Keegan seemed to have a Midas touch as manager of Newcastle and enjoyed success with Fulham and Manchester City but was never a good fit as England boss, accepting the job with misgivings and resigning after a home defeat to Germany in the last game at the old Wembley, admitting the job was beyond him. Yet only four months earlier, at Euro 2000, he had supervised England's first competitive win over the Germans since the 1966 World Cup Final.

The game is a scrappy affair, lacking quality and drama, but the result is all that matters for England, and when Alan Shearer's second-half header turns out to be the decisive moment, it sparks celebrations at home.

In the context of the Championship, though, it was meaningless: England, beaten by Portugal in their first group game, then lost to Romania and neither they nor Germany qualified for the knock-out stage.

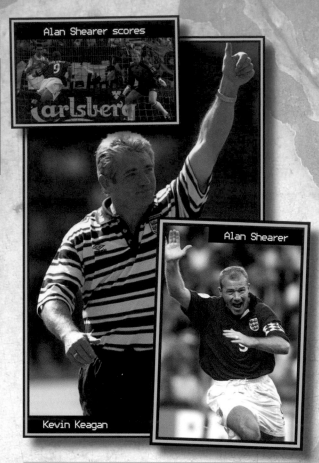
Alan Shearer scores

Alan Shearer

Kevin Keagan

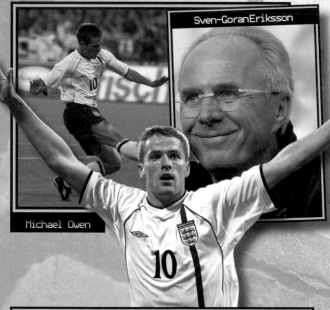
Sven-GoranEriksson

Michael Owen

Sven-Goran Eriksson (2001-06)

Germany 1 England 5

September 1, 2001; Munich;
World Cup qualifier

ERIKSSON'S RECORD

P **67** W **40** D **17** L **10**

Eriksson's 67-match reign makes him the fourth longest-serving England manager and, having reached the last eight in two World Cups and a European Championship, one of the most successful. Yet he needed only seven games to earn a place in English football folklore as England expunged the agonies of Turin and Wembley by thrashing their arch rivals in their own back yard. It was only the second home qualification match Germany had lost in their history.

Carsten Jancker puts Germany ahead after only six minutes but an inspired Michael Owen volleys a superb equaliser before Steven Gerrard's shot from 25 yards puts England in front. Early in the second half, Owen makes it 3-1 and goes on to complete the first hat-trick by an England player against Germany since Geoff Hurst's treble in the 1966 World Cup Final. Emile Heskey outpaces the home defence to drill home England's fifth.

Steven Gerrard

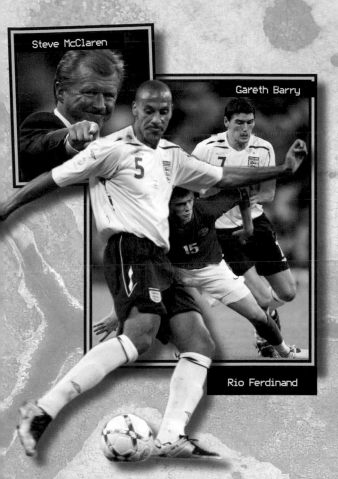

Steve McClaren

Gareth Barry

Rio Ferdinand

Steve McClaren (2006-07)

England 3 Russia 0
September 12, 2007; Wembley;
European Championship qualifier

MCCLAREN'S RECORD

P 18 W 9 D 4 L 5

McClaren's 16 months at the helm were not the happiest in England's history and his final match in charge – the home defeat to Croatia that meant England would be absent from the 2008 European Championship Finals – will haunt the former Middlesbrough manager. Yet, only two months earlier, England produced probably their best performance for McClaren during a run of five consecutive wins in the qualifying competition.

Against a strong Russian side managed by the formidable Guus Hiddink, England go ahead after seven minutes when Michael Owen scores from a cross by Gareth Barry, who dominates midfield throughout the match. After 31 minutes Owen fires home his and England's second. Rio Ferdinand adds a third six minutes from time.

Fabio Capello (2007-2012)

Croatia 1 England 4
September 10, 2008; Zagreb;
European Championship qualfier

CAPELLO'S RECORD

P 42 W 28 D 8 L 6

In many eyes, the 4-1 defeat to Germany in Bloemfontein during a poor 2010 World Cup will be recalled as the defining moment of Capello's time as England manager, even though in 42 games in charge it was one of only two defeats in competitive fixtures. England had reached the Finals by winning an impressive nine of their 10 qualification matches, laying down a marker emphatically in only the second of those, with arguably the best England performance since Eriksson's team won 5-1 in Munich in 2001, in stark contrast to the home defeat to the same opposition that had cost McClaren his job.

Apart from a couple of early scares for goalkeeper David James, England are in complete charge, with Gareth Barry a commanding figure. They go ahead on 26 minutes through a fine finish by Theo Walcott, who enjoys his best match in an England shirt, scoring twice more in the second half after Croatia's Robert Kovac is sent off. Wayne Rooney is England's other goal scorer.

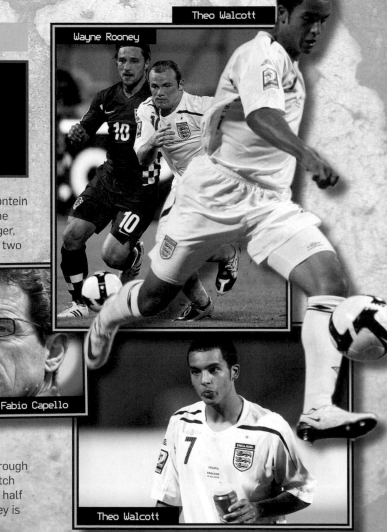

Theo Walcott

Wayne Rooney

Fabio Capello

Theo Walcott

13

20 QUESTIONS

1 Geoff Hurst famously scored a hat-trick against West Germany in the 1966 World Cup Final, but who is the only other England player to have scored three goals in a match at the World Cup Finals?

2 Since England's most successful manager, Sir Alf Ramsey, ended his stint in 1974, who has been England's longest-serving manager?

3 Who are the only two England players to be sent off twice while representing their country?

4 Other than the home nations, which countries have England played the most?

5 In 2010 Ashley Cole appeared in his third World Cup Finals. Which of these three England players have not played in three World Cup finals – Michael Owen, David Beckham or Steven Gerrard?

6 Since winning the World Cup in 1966, how many times have England reached the semi-finals of a major tournament?

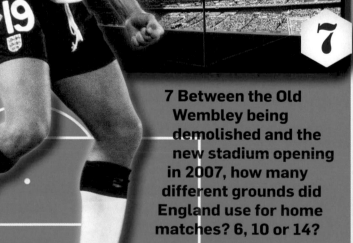

7 Between the Old Wembley being demolished and the new stadium opening in 2007, how many different grounds did England use for home matches? 6, 10 or 14?

17

8

15

8 England's 2-1 quarter-final defeat to Argentina at the 1986 World Cup is famous for Diego Maradona's two goals but who scored for England?

9 Who scored more goals for England, Paul Scholes or Paul Gascoigne?

10 Against which team did England's Euro 2012 captain Steven Gerrard make his debut?

11 Which two European nations did Roy Hodgson manage before he became England manager?

12 Which former England captain holds both the record for the fastest England goal at Wembley and the quickest England goal at the World Cup Finals?

13 Which former Arsenal defender scored England's last goal at the old Wembley Stadium?

14 Which club provided the most England players at Euro 2012?

15 Who is older, Ashley Young or Wayne Rooney?

20

16 Before Euro 2008, when was the last time England failed to qualify for a major tournament?

17 Who scored England's opening goal of the 2010 World Cup Finals?

18 Matt Le Tissier scored more than 200 goals in his career. How many were for England?

19 Who lost fewer matches as England manager, Kevin Keegan or Glenn Hoddle?

20 When did England last play old rivals Scotland — 1996, 1999 or 2002?

answers on page 61

ROAD TO RIO
FIFA World Cup in Brazil

ENGLAND'S Group H

Qualifying Campaign

Friday, September 7, 2012
MOLDOVA V ENGLAND

Tuesday, September 11, 2012
ENGLAND V UKRAINE

Friday, October 12, 2012
ENGLAND V SAN MARINO

Tuesday, October 16, 2012
POLAND V ENGLAND

Friday, March 22, 2013
SAN MARINO V ENGLAND

Tuesday, March 26, 2013
MONTENEGRO V ENGLAND

Friday, September 6, 2013
ENGLAND V MOLDOVA

Tuesday, September 10, 2013
UKRAINE V ENGLAND

Friday, October 11, 2013
ENGLAND V MONTENEGRO

Tuesday, October 15, 2013
ENGLAND V POLAND

The Finals of the 20th FIFA World Cup begin with hosts Brazil in action in Sao Paulo on Thursday, June 12, 2014, with the Final to be held on Sunday, July 13, 2014 in Rio de Janeiro.

England hope to be one of 13 qualifiers from Europe. These will be the winners of nine qualifying groups in the European zone, plus four winners from a play-off round involving the eight best runners-up.

GOALKEEPERS

Despite being universally referred to as 'Joe', Hart's first name is actually Charles, with Joseph the first of his two middle names.

The youngest England goalkeeper before Butland was Billy Moon, of the Old Westminsters and Corinthians, who was 19 years and 222 days old when he made his debut against Wales in 1888..

John is known as the 'Iceman', a nickname he picked up as a youth team player at Cambridge United because of his steely and unfazed playing style.

18

JOE HART

**Born: Shrewsbury, Shropshire
April 19, 1987**

After just two seasons as Manchester City's first choice 'keeper, Joe Hart has won The FA Cup and the Premier League, and established himself as the first name written on each England teamsheet.

Hart began his career with home-town club Shrewsbury Town and moved to City in 2006, although the 2009 arrival of Shay Given meant he had to be patient waiting for first team opportunities at Eastlands.

But, after helping Birmingham City to their highest ever Premier League finish during a loan spell at St Andrew's, the 6ft 5ins 'keeper returned to his parent club in 2010 to reclaim the number one spot.

He won the Barclays Golden Glove award in 2010-11 for the most Premier League clean sheets and was integral to the club subsequently winning their maiden Premier League crown in 2012.

After first excelling for England's Under-21s in a semi-final penalty shoot-out win over Sweden at Euro 2009, Hart has seamlessly made the transition to the senior side. He made his debut in 2008 and became a regular after the 2010 World Cup, starring for his country at Euro 2012.

JOHN RUDDY

**Born: St Ives, Cambridgeshire
October 24, 1986**

John Ruddy was frustrated to miss Euro 2012 through injury after being included in Roy Hodgson's initial 23-man squad, but the Norwich City goalkeeper can still be proud of his recent achievements.

Ruddy was named the Norfolk club's 'Players' Player of the Year' for 2011-12 after helping them to 12th place in the Premier League.

The previous season, he played in 45 of Norwich's 46 League fixtures as they won promotion from the Championship in Ruddy's first year at Carrow Road.

Before then the uncapped Ruddy, whose only previous experience with England is a brief stint in the Under-19s squad in 2005, had endured a stuttering career, making just one first team appearance in a five-year spell at Everton, during which he played for eight different clubs on loan.

That solitary appearance for the Merseyside club came in a 1-0 win over Blackburn Rovers in which he replaced the sent-off Iain Turner. Everton had paid Cambridge United £250,000 for Ruddy's services in 2005.

JACK BUTLAND

**Born: Bristol
March 10, 1993**

Butland made history in August 2012 when he became the youngest goalkeeper to represent England at senior level, stepping in because of an injury to Joe Hart to make his debut against Italy in Berne, aged 19 years and 158 days.

It followed a noteworthy summer in which he had been part of the England squad at Euro 2012, where he was called up as a late replacement for the injured John Ruddy, and then performed well as Team GB's goalkeeper in the Olympics.

Although he began the 2012-13 season as Birmingham City's first-choice keeper in the Championship, Butland's only senior experience before his full international and Olympic involvement came during a loan spell with Cheltenham Town in League Two.

A product of the Birmingham City Academy, which he joined as a 14-year-old, Butland has been involved with England at every level from Under-16s upwards and was a part of the squad which lifted the UEFA European Under-17 Championship in Liechtenstein in May 2010, and was first-choice 'keeper for the Under-21s in 2011-12.

ROAD TO RIO

Spotlight on England's opponents in Qualifying Group H

Moldova

HEAD TO HEAD
England   2 wins
Moldova   0 wins
Draws 0

Friday, September 7, 2012
MOLDOVA V ENGLAND

Friday, September 6, 2013
ENGLAND V MOLDOVA

A former Soviet state, Moldova have been vying for qualification for major tournaments since 1994 but have never seriously threatened to achieve that goal. England should have little to fear from a country with only a handful of competitive victories to their name.

Their Euro 2012 qualifying campaign was boosted only by two victories over San Marino while Moldova claimed no victories at all in attempting to reach the 2010 World Cup in South Africa, failing even to beat Luxembourg over two games.

Very few of Moldova's players play outside eastern Europe, their most capped player Radu Rebeja and top goalscorer Serghei Clescenco, who has netted 11 times for his country, being two prime examples. One of Moldova's biggest stars, Stanislav Ivanov, is currently a free agent after being released by Lokomotiv Moscow in 2011.

The last time the countries were drawn together in a qualifying group, England won 3-0 in Chisinau and 4-0 at home en route to the France '98 World Cup Finals, with Paul Gascoigne on target in both games. England will hope to register similarly commanding victories in this campaign.

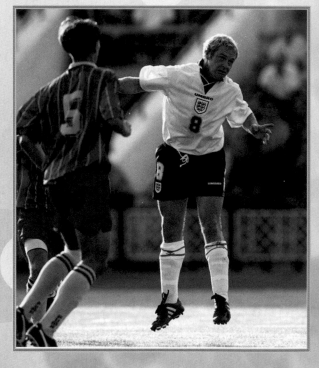

The England team in history – 100 years ago

The first official international football match took place between England and Scotland in Glasgow in 1872 but it was a long time before the England team began to venture beyond the United Kingdom, largely because there was no air travel and the standard of continental opposition did not offer much of a challenge.

England were largely limited to playing against Wales, Scotland and the then-united Ireland, who in time competed for an annual British Home Championship. Scotland would regularly beat England in the early years, in contrast to Ireland, who had to wait until the 13th meeting between the sides before managing even to draw.

So imagine the celebrations on February 15, 1913, when a 20,000 crowd at Windsor Park, Belfast, finally witnessed an Ireland victory.

It came at the 32nd time of asking, after 28 defeats and three draws, and against the odds after an injury to their inside left, James McAuley, shortly after England took a 10th-minute lead. There were no substitutes in those days, so Ireland were reduced to 10 men.

Having gone in front with a goal by Charlie Buchan, the Sunderland star making his debut, England must have expected another emphatic scoreline but the Irish fought like Tigers and another debutant, the Sheffield United forward Billy Gillespie, scored twice to give them an historic win.

The game ended in chaos. With still three minutes left, the referee blew for a free kick but large numbers in the crowd thought it was the final whistle, surging on to the field and carrying their heroes aloft. There was no chance of restarting the game, yet the result was allowed to stand.

Euro 2012 stats and results

Quarter-Finals

Czech Republic 0 Portugal 1 Ronaldo 79

Germany 4 Greece 2 Lahm 39, Khedira 61, Klose 68, Reus 74, Samaras 55, Salpingidis pen 89

Spain 2 France 0 Alonso 19, 90(pen)

England 0 Italy 0 (Italy won 4-2 on penalties)

Semi-Finals

Portugal 0 Spain 0 (Spain won 4-2 on penalties)

Germany 1 Italy 2 Ozil 90 (pen), Balotelli 20, 36"

Final

Spain 4 Italy 0 Silva 14, Alba 41, Torres 84, Mata 88
Golden Boot Fernando Torres (Spain) 3 goals, Mario Balotelli (Italy), Mario Gomez (Germany), Mario Mandzukic (Croatia), Cristiano Ronaldo (Portugal) and Alan Dzagoev (Russia) also scored 3 goals. Torres also finished level with Gomez on goals and assists, the next determining factor, but won the Golden Boot because he played fewer minutes.

UEFA Team of the Tournament

Goalkeepers – Gianluigi Buffon (Italy), Manuel Neuer (Germany), Iker Casillas (Spain)

Defenders – Phillip Lahm (Germany), Fabio Coentrao, Pepe (both Portugal), Jordi Alba, Gerard Pique, Sergio Ramos (all Spain)

Midfielders – Steven Gerrard (England), Sami Khedira, Mezut Ozil (both Germany), Andrea Pirlo, Daniele De Rossi (both Italy), Xabi Alonso, Sergio Busquets, Xavi, Andres Iniesta (all Spain)

Forwards – Mario Balotelli (Italy), Cristiano Ronaldo (Portugal), Zlatan Ibrahimovic (Sweden), Cesc Fabregas, David Silva (both Spain)

UEFA Player of the Tournament Andres Iniesta (Spain)

Penalty agony again ends England's hopes

England 0-0 Italy (Italy won 4-2 on penalties)

Roy Hodgson's first tournament as manager brought enormous credit for a gallant effort by England to reach the quarter-finals of Euro 2012 in Poland and Ukraine.

But penalties – the national team's downfall now in three World Cups and three European championships -- once again provided the ultimate pain as Italy won a shoot-out to advance to the semi-finals.

The Italians, for whom Andrea Pirlo provided so much creativity, probably merited progression after squandering a number of chances in 90 minutes and extra time.

England were not without a threat, with Glen Johnson and Danny Welbeck missing opportunities in the first half of normal time, but they faded as the match progressed.

Daniele De Rossi inexplicably dragged Italy's best chance wide from close range, while Mario Balotelli had a shot blocked by John Terry after being played through in the first half and was denied by Joe Hart from close range in the second.

Riccardo Montolivo volleyed over while substitute Antonio Nocerino looked to have won it for Italy, finally, when he headed in with five minutes to play in extra time, only to be denied by the offside flag.

By this stage England's attacking potential had been limited to hopeful set pieces and they played out the draw to reach penalties.

But after making the perfect start when Steven Gerrard and Wayne Rooney converted and Montolivo dragged his penalty wide, Ashley Young's spot kick struck the bar.

Pirlo had cheekily chipped Italy level in the shoot-out before Young's failure, which was compounded when Ashley Cole's tame effort was parried to safety by Buffon after Nocerino had put Italy 3-2 ahead.

Former West Ham forward Alessandro Diamanti was the man charged with putting Italy through and he made no mistake, breaking English hearts in the process.

Italy's players roared with delight and charged forwards while England's sank to their knees in despair. It was a cruel end to a match, and a tournament, in which England had fought hard.

Roy Hodgson could take pride that his team had not lost a match in 90 minutes but the mesmeric way in which Italy retained possession where England struggled to keep the ball was one reason why England's players were so tired at the end.

They had covered a lot of ground and withstood a barrage of attacks merely to arrive at their dreaded nemesis – penalties.

England had gone out of the Italia '90, France '98 and Germany 2002 World Cups via the lottery of a shoot-out, and can now add Euro 2012 to a catalogue of heartbreaks that also includes, of course, Euro '96 on home soil, as well as the 2004 Euros in Portugal.

The last time England played Italy in a competitive fixture – in the final qualifying match for the France '98 World Cup – the score was also 0-0. The result gave England an automatic place in the Finals and is remembered as one of the national team's greatest performances in recent history. This scoreless draw in Kiev will not be remembered as fondly.

Euro 2012 Review

The Group Stages

England 1 France 1
June 11, 2012; Donbass Arena, Donetsk (Ukraine)
Goals: Lescott (30) 1-0; Nasri (39) 1-1

Joleon Lescott's first-half header helped England to a draw with France in their opening match in Group D.

The Manchester City defender converted Steven Gerrard's teasing delivery to give England a 1-0 advantage in Donetsk although Samir Nasri equalised for France before half-time.

Sterling second-half performances from both teams were not enough to register any further score although Roy Hodgson was encouraged to see his team more than match a French side who came into the tournament boasting an impressive 21-match unbeaten run.

England manager Hodgson sprang surprises with his team

selection, including 18 year-old Alex Oxlade-Chamberlain and playing a lone striker in Danny Welbeck.

The French enjoyed the bulk of possession but lacked potency in attack, creating few clear chances. Star striker Karim Benzema often dropped deep and failed to stretch England's defence often enough.

James Milner might have given England an early lead but could only find the side netting after cleverly rounding goalkeeper Hugo Lloris. Lescott then did nod England ahead but Manchester City midfielder Nasri's superb strike from the edge of the penalty area meant England held the advantage for just 9 minutes.

A cagey second half produced few opportunities and the match petered out into a draw with Manchester United's Welbeck performing with maturity in his isolated role up front.

Teams

England (4-4-1-1): Hart; Johnson, Terry, Lescott, Cole; Milner, Gerrard, Parker (Henderson 77), Oxlade-Chamberlain (Defoe 77); Young; Welbeck (Walcott 90).
Yellow cards: Oxlade-Chamberlain, Young.

France (4-5-1): Lloris; Debuchy, Rami, Mexes, Evra; Nasri, Cabaye (Martin 84), Diarra, Malouda (Ben Arfa 84), Ribery; Benzema.

England 3-2 Sweden
June 15, 2012; Olympic Stadium, Kiev (Ukraine)
Goals: Carroll (23) 1-0; Johnson o.g. (49) 1-1; Mellberg (59) 1-2; Walcott (64) 2-2; Welbeck (78) 3-2.

Roy Hodgson's team were staring at a potentially disastrous defeat before coming from behind to beat Sweden in Kiev and leave themselves in prime position to qualify for the knock-out stages.

England trailed 2-1 early in the second half after a Swedish response spearheaded by Olaf Mellberg had overturned the lead Andy Carroll's header had given the Three Lions.

But a deflected effort from substitute Theo Walcott, who transformed the match after coming on, and a cute close-range finish from Danny Welbeck gave England a thrilling victory in Ukraine's capital.

Carroll's 23rd-minute opener was just reward for England as they began the match with purpose. The Liverpool forward had been recalled so England could play an extra striker, a decision which proved

sound thinking as the tall man powered in a pinpoint cross from Steven Gerrard.

Sweden only briefly threatened in the first half, with John Terry and Joleon Lescott effectively marshalling star man Zlatan Ibrahimovic.

From nowhere, however, the match was turned on its head in the opening 15 minutes of the second half. Former Aston Villa defender Mellberg first had a close range shot deflected in off Glen Johnson

24

before rising unmarked to head in Sunderland winger Seb Larsson's free kick. Walcott's pace gave England an extra weapon after his introduction and, after equalising himself in the 64th minute, he set up Welbeck for England's winner 12 minutes from time.

Teams

England (4-4-?)·
Hart; Johnson, Terry, Lescott, Cole; Milner (Walcott 60), Gerrard, Parker, Young; Welbeck (Oxlade-Chamberlain 89), Carroll.
Yellow card: Milner.

Sweden (4-4-1-1): Isaksson; Granqvist, Mellberg, J Olsson, M Olsson; Larsson, Svensson, Kallstrom, Elm; Ibrahimovic; Elmander.

England 1 Ukraine 0
June 19, 2012; Donbass Arena, Donetsk (Ukraine)
Goal: Rooney (48) 1-0.

Wayne Rooney scored on his return from suspension to end the hopes of co-hosts Ukraine and send England through to the quarter-finals as group winners.

The Manchester United striker found space at the back post to head into an empty net early in the second half after Steven Gerrard's cross had evaded several scrambling bodies.

Ukraine rallied after this, lighting up what had been a largely sedate encounter, and should have equalised when Marko Devic's shot was partially saved by Joe Hart before John Terry desperately hooked the ball clear. Replays seemed to show the ball had crossed the line.

Rooney had by far the clearest chance of the first half, glancing a free header wide after a pinpoint cross from Ashley Young had found him in space.

Ukraine showed gusto and bravery in attack, roared on by the partisan and vociferous home support, and the promising Andriy Yarmolenko could have soon put his team ahead.

After Rooney's goal and Devic's 'ghost' goal – which England will feel offered a measure of justice after the Frank Lampard goal that was not given against Germany at the 2010 World Cup – England's defence had to hold firm in the face of waves of attacks from the host nation.

Ashley Cole could have sealed England's win late on but was denied by 'keeper Andriy Pyatov and even Ukrainian talisman Andriy Shevchenko was unable to inspire a comeback from his country after coming on as a substitute.

Teams

England (4-4-2): Hart; Johnson, Terry, Lescott, Cole; Milner (Walcott 70), Gerrard, Parker, Young; Rooney (Oxlade-Chamberlain 87), Welbeck (Carroll 82).
Yellow cards: Cole, Gerrard.

Ukraine (4-1-2-3): Pyatov; Gusev, Khacheridi, Rakitskiy, Selin; Tymoshchuk; Yarmolenko, Konoplyanka; Garmash (Nazarenko 78), Milevskiy (Butko 77), Devic (Shevchenko 70).
Yellow cards: Tymoshchuk, Rakitskiy, Shevchenko.

Euro 2012 stats and results

Group A

Results	Table	P	W	D	L	GF	GA	Pts	GD
Poland 1-1 Greece	1 Czech Republic	3	2	0	1	4	5	6	-1
Russia 4-1 Czech Republic	2 Greece	3	1	1	1	3	3	4	0
Greece 1-2 Czech Republic	3 Russia	3	1	1	1	5	3	4	+2
Poland 1-1 Russia	4 Poland	3	0	2	1	2	3	2	-1
Czech Republic 1-0 Poland									
Greece 1-0 Russia									

(Greece finished above Russia by virtue of the teams' head-to-head record)

Group B

Results	Table	P	W	D	L	GF	GA	Pts	GD
Netherlands 0-1 Denmark	1 Germany	3	3	0	0	5	2	9	+3
Germany 1-0 Portugal	2 Portugal	3	2	0	1	5	4	6	+1
Denmark 2-3 Portugal	3 Denmark	3	1	0	2	4	5	3	-1
Netherlands 1-2 Germany	4 Netherlands	3	0	0	3	2	5	0	-3
Portugal 2-1 Netherlands									
Denmark 1-2 Germany									

Group C

Results	Table	P	W	D	L	GF	GA	Pts	GD
Spain 1-1 Italy	1 Spain	3	2	1	0	6	1	7	+5
Rep of Ireland 1-3 Croatia	2 Italy	3	1	2	0	4	2	5	+2
Italy 1-1 Croatia	3 Croatia	3	1	1	1	4	3	4	+1
Spain 4-0 Republic of Ireland	4 Rep of Ireland	3	0	0	3	1	9	0	-8
Croatia 0-1 Spain									
Italy 2-0 Rep of Ireland									

Group D

Results	Table	P	W	D	L	GF	GA	Pts	GD
France 1-1 England	1 England	3	2	1	0	5	3	7	+2
Ukraine 2-1 Sweden	2 France	3	1	1	1	3	3	4	0
Ukraine 0-2 France	3 Ukraine	3	1	0	2	2	4	3	-2
Sweden 2-3 England	4 Sweden	3	1	0	2	5	5	3	0
England 1-0 Ukraine									
Sweden 2-0 France									

(Ukraine finished above Sweden by virtue of the teams' head-to-head record)

Spain reign again

In the end, it was Spain's golden generation who won an unprecedented third consecutive major trophy, saving their best performance at Euro 2012 until last.

The manner in which they dismantled Italy underlined the superb versatility of the current crop of Spanish attacking stars in a line-up that did not include a recognised striker.

David Silva and the irrepressible Andres Iniesta, who scored the winning goal in the 2010 World Cup Final, were sublime throughout, and the latter was named UEFA's Player of the Tournament. Goals from Silva, Jordi Alba, Fernando Torres and Juan Mata earned Spain a deserved and comprehensive victory.

In the group stage, Spain drew with Italy before dispatching Ireland and edging out Croatia to reach the knockout stage and two Xabi Alonso goals were enough to see off a limp French team in the quarter-finals. France had begun promisingly against England and co-hosts Ukraine but surprisingly lost to Sweden in their last group game to finish only second and rarely threatened Spain, who were defending the crown they won at Euro 2008.

Only when a Cristiano Ronaldo-inspired Portugal took them to penalties in a goalless semi-final was Spain's dominance challenged, but they held their nerve to survive the shoot-out.

To progress from Group B, the so-called 'group of death', the Portuguese had recovered from an opening loss to Germany to beat Denmark 3-2 and inflicted a 2-1 defeat on a disappointing Holland, who were among the pre-tournament favourites but lost all three games.

Ronaldo scored a quarter-final winner for Portugal against the Czech Republic, who won Group A with wins over Greece and co-hosts Poland despite being trounced by Russia in their first game. Greece beat Russia in the final game to go through with them.

In the quarter-finals, Greece were soundly beaten by Germany, who won Group B with three wins out of three and were fancied to win the tournament only for the Italians, who they have never beaten in a competitive match, again to be their undoing.

Italy were not expected to shine at Euro 2012 and they needed a narrow win over Ireland to squeeze past Croatia into second place in Group D.

But they scaled new heights in the knock-out stages, the mesmeric Andrea Pirlo helping them break English hearts in the quarter-finals before Mario Balotelli struck twice to earn his country a momentous semi-final win over Germany. Yet the bigger test that awaited Italy in the Final was one they never looked like passing.

Spain remain the greatest team in Europe, by some distance. If they can win the 2014 World Cup in Brazil – and by doing so become the first European team to win the tournament in South America – they will have a claim to be seen as the best team in history.

DEFENDERS

JOHN TERRY

Born: Barking, London
December 7, 1980

Despite suspension ruling him out of the Final, John Terry was able – after several near misses – to add the 2012 Champions League to his collection of honours when Chelsea beat Bayern Munich on penalties in the German side's own Allianz Arena in May. Yet his heroic efforts were not enough to complete an unlikely double with England at Euro 2012, meaning a major international tournament victory continues to elude him.

One of the most celebrated English footballers of his generation, central defender Terry has spent his entire senior career at Stamford Bridge, bar a brief loan spell with Nottingham Forest in 2000, and is the club's most successful captain of all time, also winning three Premier League titles, four FA Cups and two League Cups.

Regarded as a natural leader, Terry also captained England under both Steve McLaren and Fabio Capello and attracts regular praise for his brave and wholehearted defending. He won the PFA's 'Players' Player of the Year Award' in 2005.

The Londoner has competed in four major tournaments for England. At 6ft 1ins, he can also pose an attacking threat in the air, especially at set-pieces. His goals for his country include the first international goal at the new Wembley Stadium in 2007.

Did you know?
John played in midfield for West Ham United as a boy and became a defender at Chelsea only because of a shortage of central defenders at the club.

ASHLEY COLE

Born: Stepney, London
December 20, 1980

Did you know?
Euro 2012 was the first major tournament that Ashley was the only 'Cole' included in the England squad. Joe, Andrew and Carlton have also played for England during Ashley's international career.

penalty miss in the shoot-out against Italy marred an otherwise solid showing, he was two away from becoming only the sixth England player to win 100 caps.

Cole was an established star with Arsenal before he completed a controversial move across London to Stamford Bridge in 2006. He was a member of the Gunners' 'Invincibles' team, and has since won all three domestic trophies and the Champions League as a Chelsea player.

Despite the exuberance with which he goes forward on overlapping runs, Cole is not known for his goalscoring prowess, yet is usually a reliable penalty-taker and scored in Chelsea's 2012 Champions League Final shoot-out victory over Bayern Munich.

After Chelsea's heroic Champions League triumph, Ashley Cole can now use a complete list of club honours to justify arguments that he is the best left-back in world football.

England's most capped full-back, Cole has been virtually an ever-present since his 2001 debut, playing in five major tournaments. He won huge praise for his performance against Portugal's brilliant Cristiano Ronaldo at the 2006 World Cup and was integral to England's strong showing at Euro 2004. At the end of Euro 2012, when his

Glen Johnson

Born: Greenwich, London
August 23, 1984

Glen Johnson has blossomed into England's first-choice right-back since moving to Liverpool, having made just 41 appearances in a four-year spell at Roman Abramovich's Chelsea.

The defender was the Russian's first signing as Chelsea supremo, arriving from West Ham United in 2003, but Johnson's career at Stamford Bridge was a truncated one. He had a season-long loan at Portsmouth in 2006-07, which led to a permanent move the following year, finally giving him regular first team football.

Known for his strength and pace, Johnson shone at Fratton Park, helping the Hampshire club to win The FA Cup in 2008, which completed his set of domestic honours, after he claimed Premier League and League Cup winners' medals at Chelsea.

The Londoner's fine form at Portsmouth attracted several prospective suitors, and it was Liverpool that won the race to sign Johnson, paying £18m to take him to Anfield. After injury initially stalled his progress at Liverpool, Johnson has come back stronger and, despite mixed fortunes in the Premier League, helped the Reds win the 2012 Carling Cup.

Johnson made his senior England debut in 2003 when just 19 years old and succeeded Gary Neville as first-choice right-back towards the end of his time with Portsmouth. A solid showing in the 2010 World Cup qualifying campaign cemented his position and he scored his first goal for his country in a warm-up match for that tournament against Mexico in May 2010.

Leighton Baines

Born: Kirkby, Merseyside
December 11, 1984

The ever-consistent Leighton Baines has become the first-choice understudy to Ashley Cole at left-back for England after forging an excellent career in the north-west.

The left back moved to Everton from Wigan in 2007, and has produced displays of sufficient class to warrant international recognition.

The Liverpudlian, who actually supported Liverpool as a boy, was an integral member of the Wigan team which rose from the lower leagues to the top flight, winning the Second Division (now League One) title in his first full season and helping the Latics to promotion to the Premier League in 2005.

The 28-year-old helped Wigan reach the 2006 Carling Cup Final in their first season in the top flight, before he secured a £5million move to Goodison Park. He played in the FA Cup Final with Everton in 2009, made his senior England debut against Egypt at Wembley in 2010 and was named Everton's 2010-11 'Player of the Season'.

While far from a prolific goalscorer, Baines is a useful penalty-taker and capable of delivering outstanding quality from free kicks, one of which won Everton's 2011 'Goal of the Season' award.

Capped 16 times at Under-21 level, Baines was unlucky to miss the 2010 World Cup but was included in Roy Hodgson's 23-man squad at Euro 2012.

DEFENDERS

Phil Jagielka

**Born: Sale,
Greater Manchester
August 17, 1982**

Having helped Sheffield United win promotion to the Premier League in 2006, defender Phil Jagielka has never played outside the top flight since and is now a regular feature of England senior squads.

The Cheshire-born centre-half originally played in central midfield at Bramall Lane where his tough tackling style and spectacular goals established him as a fans' favourite.

Jagielka possesses an exceptional footballing brain and has even been deployed as an emergency goalkeeper. Neil Warnock rarely named a substitute 'keeper when he was manager at Sheffield United because of Jagielka's prowess wearing the gloves.

DID YOU KNOW?
Before opting to represent England at international level, Phil could have played for Poland, qualifying through his Polish-born grandfather Nikodem, from whom he takes his middle name.

Since making a £4m move to Merseyside in 2007, the 28-year-old has largely concentrated his efforts on being a defender and he has become a potent aerial threat going forward. He also helped the Toffees to the 2009 FA Cup Final, scoring the winning penalty against Manchester United in the semi-final, and was Everton's 'Player of the Year' in the same season.

Jagielka made his first senior England start five years after winning the last of his six Under-21 caps, playing in the 3-0 win over Trinidad & Tobago in 2008.

Kyle Walker

**Born: Sheffield
May 28, 1990**

DID YOU KNOW?
Despite leaving Sheffield United for the glitz and glamour of the Premier League, Kyle remains a fervent supporter of his boyhood club, still attending Blades matches when his schedule allows him to.

Walker did not become a first team regular at White Hart Lane until 2011, after enjoying three successful spells out on loan, first with former club Sheffield United and then Queen's Park Rangers and Aston Villa, but has now become an integral component of Tottenham's team.

Injury may have denied Kyle Walker the opportunity to play in his first major international tournament at Euro 2012, but the promising Tottenham full-back appears to have a long England future ahead of him after some excellent domestic performances.

The Yorkshire-born defender began his career at Sheffield United, where his pace and talent prompted Spurs to sign him after making just seven appearances for the Blades, one of which was the 2009 Championship Play-Off Final at Wembley.

His sterling efforts in the 2011-12 season earned him the PFA's 'Young Player of the Year Award' and his first senior England caps. Walker started for the national team for the first time against Sweden at Wembley in November 2011.

The Spurs man also made seven international appearances at both Under-19 and Under-21 level, being named in the 'Team of the Tournament' at the 2011 European Under-21 Championship.

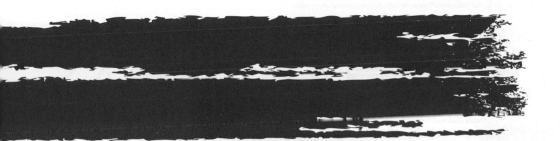

Chris Smalling
Born: Greenwich, London
November 22, 1989

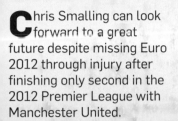

Chris Smalling can look forward to a great future despite missing Euro 2012 through injury after finishing only second in the 2012 Premier League with Manchester United.

The Londoner is equally adept at right-back as he is in the centre of defence and this versatility persuaded Sir Alex Ferguson to pay Fulham £8m to bring Smalling to Manchester United in 2010.

Smalling had made only 13 first team appearances for the West London club, but has grown in stature since moving to Manchester, scoring his first League goal for the club against

Chelsea in 2011.

In just two seasons at Old Trafford, the defender has won the 2011 Premier League and been involved in the Champions League Final of the same year, which augurs well for his future prospects of winning trophies.

Smalling made his England debut against Bulgaria in Sofia in 2011, having played 14 times at Under-21 level. He scored the winning goal against Romania in a European Championship play-off in 2010.

Chris agreed terms with Middlesbrough in 2008 before joining Fulham but cancelled his contract at the Riverside Stadium soon after moving to the north-east because of homesickness.

Gary Cahill
Born: Sheffield
December 19, 1985

A full England international and a Champions League winner with Chelsea, Gary Cahill has come a long way since being deemed surplus to requirements at Aston Villa in 2008.

The central defender began his career at Villa but found opportunities limited in Birmingham, although he earned a lasting place in affections of Villa fans with his solitary goal for the club – a spectacular bicycle kick in a Second City derby win over Birmingham City.

Since moving to Bolton in 2008 his career has flourished. At the end of the 2011-12 season, he was close to 150 appearances for Wanderers, having helped ensure there would be Premier League status at the Reebok Stadium for a fourth season in a row.

His efforts for Bolton won him his first England caps, after playing for his country at both Under-20 and Under-21 levels, and earned him an exciting move to Chelsea, where he has already won FA

Cup and Champions League winners' medals.

The 6ft 2ins defender first played for England against Bulgaria at Wembley in 2010 and scored for his nation for the first time against the same country a year later.

Only injury deprived him of a place in Roy Hodgson's 23-man squad at Euro 2012.

Level-headed on the pitch and grounded in his personality, Gary still regularly visits AFC Dronfield, the club from the Derbyshire town just south of Sheffield where he played his first serious football.

DEFENDERS

Joleon Lescott

Born: Quinton, Birmingham
August 16, 1982

Joleon Lescott will hope to make a berth in the centre of defence his own after proving a pivotal figure for England at Euro 2012 – his first major tournament – when Roy Hodgson's side did not lose a single match in 90 minutes.

The Birmingham-born player was plying his trade in the Championship with Wolves as recently as 2006 but has now established an international career as well as winning the Premier League title with Manchester City.

After helping Wolves win promotion to the Premier League in 2004, Lescott missed the entire 2004-05 Premier League season through injury and Wolves were relegated before he had chance to experience playing in the top flight.

But that chance came with his move to Everton in 2006 and he produced a host of consistent performances, earning his first England cap while with the Merseyside club – against Estonia in 2007 – before Manchester City secured his services in 2010 in a deal reportedly worth £24m.

Lescott can be a potent threat from set pieces, scoring 17 times in his four-year spell at Everton.

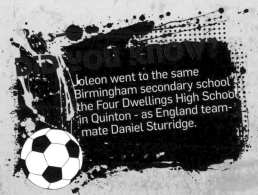

Joleon went to the same Birmingham secondary school, the Four Dwellings High School in Quinton - as England team-mate Daniel Sturridge.

Blackburn Rovers had the foresight to protect themselves financially from losing Phil. When he was only 18, they inserted a clause into his contract allowing him to leave only for a minimum transfer fee of £16m.

Phil Jones

Born: Preston
February 21, 1992

Destined for stardom from an early age, Phil Jones has already commanded a transfer fee in excess of £16m despite the majority of his career still lying ahead of him.

The Manchester United man joined Blackburn Rovers' youth system in 2002 at the age of 10 and broke into the Lancashire club's first team at the age of 17. He made his Premier League debut just after turning 18 and soon established himself in the heart of Blackburn's defence.

Since completing a lucrative transfer to Old Trafford in 2011, Jones has proved equally adept in a defensive midfield position and has also played at full-back for Sir Alex Ferguson's team.

A more skilful ball player than the average defender, Jones also caught the eye of Fabio Capello, who gave him his full England debut in the final Euro 2012 qualifier in Montenegro in October.

His first season at Manchester United did not yield any trophies despite the club going agonisingly close to the Premier League title, although his performances were enough to ensure his inclusion in England's 23-man squad for Euro 2012.

ROAD TO RIO

Spotlight on England's opponents in Qualifying Group H

Ukraine

HEAD TO HEAD
England	4 wins
Ukraine	1 wins
Draws 0	

Tuesday, Sept 11, 2012
ENGLAND V UKRAINE

Tuesday, Sept 10, 2013
UKRAINE V ENGLAND

England will be wary of a Ukraine team seeking revenge after Roy Hodgson's side proved the ultimate party-poopers for the former Soviet state at Euro 2012. Ukraine, co-hosts of the tournament, were evicted from their own shindig losing 1-0 to England in Donetsk and they will be determined to compete in a major tournament again in 2014.

England are due to return to Ukraine in September, 2013 when their hosts will hope still to be in contention for qualification. Since gaining independence from the USSR, Ukraine have qualified for only one major tournament – they didn't need to at Euro 2012 – but they did make the quarter-finals of the 2006 World Cup in Germany, losing to eventual winners Italy.

Talismanic former Chelsea striker Andriy Shevchenko announced his retirement from international football after Euro 2012, but Dynamo Kiev's young forward Andriy Yarmolenko will pose a danger to England after impressing in the Finals in Poland and Ukraine, while veterans Anatoliy Tymoshchuk and Andriy Voronin should continue to provide valuable experience.

Their Euro 2012 co-hosts Poland will probably be Ukraine's chief rivals for qualification, in addition to England, and they can take comfort from their relatively strong World Cup qualifying record; they have won 23 qualifiers – including a 1-0 success over England in Kiev in 2009 – and lost only eight.

By the 1930s, England would most years embark on an end-of-season tour in mainland Europe, but this landed them in enormous controversy on May 14, 1938 when the first match of the tour, against Germany in Berlin, was seized by Adolf Hitler as a showcase for Nazi propaganda.

While the England players were getting changed an FA official went into their dressing-room and told them that they had to make the Nazi salute during the playing of the German national anthem. The request did not go down well with the players. News of Hitler's rise had made many in Britain uncomfortable and the England team made it clear they did not want to be involved with any political gestures.

The FA official left but returned with a direct order from the British Ambassador, Sir Neville Henderson, that the players must make the salute because of the sensitivity of relations between Britain and Germany and the fear that it needed "only a spark to set Europe alight".

Reluctantly the England team raised their right arms, with the exception of Stan Cullis, who refused and was subsequently dropped from the squad.

Hitler, who disliked football, did not attend but among a crowd of 110,000 people were senior Nazis Hermann Göring and Joseph Goebbels.

The German team had been selected after months of trials and trained for 10 days at a camp in the Black Forest, but in the event were no match for England, who won the game 6-3, with goals from Cliff Bastin, Jackie Robinson (2), Frank Broome, Stanley Matthews and Len Goulden, whose 25-yard volley was described by Matthews as the best goal he had ever seen.

Allen, the official match ball of the 1938 FIFA World Cup in France

BOBBY CHARLTON TRIBUTE

> 66 **England beat us because Bobby Charlton was better than me** 99
>
> Franz Beckenbauer

1966 who was awarded his World Cup medal in 2009, share the distinction.

Sir Bobby won 106 England caps, the fourth highest tally in history, and scored 49 goals, which is the highest total achieved by an England player, one more than Gary Lineker. But he is renowned just as much for the spirit in which he played the game, a gentleman on the field with respect for officials and opponents and, above all, football itself.

Born in Ashington, Northumberland in 1937, Charlton signed for Manchester United on June 1, 1953 and until he became manager of Preston North End in 1973 it was his only club.

He survived the dreadful tragedy of the Munich air disaster, which claimed the lives of eight of his United team-mates, and went on to score a club record 249 goals, winning three League titles, an FA Cup and, in 1968, the European Cup, as United beat Benfica 4-1 at Wembley.

Charlton scored the first and fourth goals in a victory that established him as an all-time great, coming two years after another great Wembley occasion and another glorious moment in his career, the 2-1 defeat of Portugal that put England in the World Cup Final. In a performance some described as the best of his international career, a master class that ran the Portuguese ragged, he scored both England's goals.

And while Geoff Hurst stole the headlines in the Final, the German great Franz Beckenbauer credits Charlton as the man who inspired the victory. Given the job of limiting Charlton's influence as best he could, Beckenbauer conceded later that he came out second best. "England beat us because Bobby Charlton was better than me," he said.

Charlton was made an OBE in 1969, a CBE in 1974 and was knighted in 1994.

O f almost 1,200 players to have worn the Three Lions since the first England team met Scotland in 1872, none is more famous arguably than Sir Bobby Charlton, who celebrated his 75th birthday in 2012 and in 2013 will mark 60 years since he signed his first professional contract. His achievements in the game are matched only by his own modesty.

An attacking midfielder of graceful fluency on the ball and packing a thunderously powerful shot, Charlton is one of a select group of players who have winners' medals from both the World Cup and the European Cup. Among England players, only his Manchester United team-mate Nobby Stiles and the Liverpool winger Ian Callaghan, a squad member in

106 Caps

49 Goals for England

249 Club Goals

MIDFIELDERS

Steven Gerrard

Born: Whiston, Merseyside; May 30, 1980

While Euro 2012 ended disappointingly, Steven Gerrard will have been extremely proud to have captained his country throughout the tournament.

Having skippered Liverpool since 2003, nobody could dispute that Gerrard deserved the accolade Roy Hodgson awarded him and he thrived on the responsibility, setting up three of his country's goals en route to being named in UEFA's Team of the Tournament.

The talismanic midfielder made his debut for England against Ukraine in May 2000, a day after his 20th birthday, and his first goal for his country helped England to a famous 5-1 victory over Germany in Munich.

Gerrard missed the 2002 World Cup through injury, but has been involved at five major tournaments with England, including three quarter-final exits, the first two coming against Portugal in 2004 and 2006 and the third being last summer's defeat to Italy.

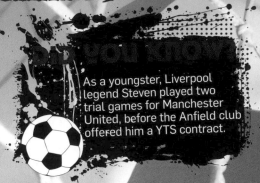

As a youngster, Liverpool legend Steven played two trial games for Manchester United, before the Anfield club offered him a YTS contract.

The Premier League, which Liverpool crave more than any other trophy having not been crowned English Champions since 1990, has eluded Gerrard so far but he has achieved almost everything else with his hometown club.

Last year's Carling Cup triumph brought Gerrard his seventh major trophy in club football. His greatest night was undoubtedly when he inspired Liverpool to Champions League glory in 2005, helping them claw back a 3-0 deficit against AC Milan in the Final before winning on penalties.

The 2006 FA Cup Final against West Ham will also be remembered for Gerrard's telling contributions. Having already equalised once for Liverpool, he lashed home an unstoppable strike from 35 yards out to haul his team level for a second time at 3-3 in injury time, before they went on to win on penalties.

A dynamic, tough-tackling midfielder, Gerrard's consistently accurate passing means he is usually deployed in central midfield but his attacking prowess and goal threat sees him frequently play just behind a lone striker.

Stewart Downing

Born: Middlesbrough; July 24, 1984

Stewart Downing's first full season at Liverpool following his 2011 switch to Anfield was perhaps not as successful as he had hoped, although the former Aston Villa winger was virtually an ever present in the first team and his performances earned him a berth in Roy Hodgson's squad for Euro 2012. The 28-year-old started playing at hometown club Middlesbrough, with whom he won the 2004 League Cup and

reached the UEFA Cup Final two years later. When the north-east outfit were relegated in 2009, Aston Villa were Downing's next port of call, and his superb season in 2010-11 – in which he scored eight goals – prompted Liverpool to pay the Birmingham club around £20m for his services.

Some feel Downing should make more of his goal-scoring ability but his creative talent is irrefutable. He can play on either wing although he is largely reliant on his left foot, and has the ability to deliver teasing crosses or dribble past defenders by using a clever turn of pace.

The Liverpool midfielder played seven times for England's Under-21s, and despite having never forged a regular place in the senior team, he has been selected by four different England managers.

Ashley Young

Born: Stevenage; July 9, 1985

Manchester United's Ashley Young has proved he has a strong temperament, which will surely see him quickly recover from his penalty miss for England against Italy at Euro 2012.

The Hertfordshire-born midfielder coped with huge expectations last year to make a strong impression in an injury-hit first season at Old Trafford, having moved north after spending four years at Aston Villa, where he helped the club to successive sixth-placed finishes in 2008 and 2009.

Young's devastating right foot and eye for goal first came to prominence under Aidy Boothroyd's stewardship at Watford, who he helped win promotion to the Premier League in 2006. The Hornets initially rejected Young for being too small but youth coach Chris Cummins persuaded them to persevere with him and they were right to heed his advice, eventually receiving nearly £10m from Villa for him in 2007.

Young appeared for England at Under-21 level 10 times before he made his senior debut against Austria in 2007. He scored his first England goal in a friendly against Denmark in February 2011 and went on to play a pivotal role in helping England qualify for Euro 2012, scoring against Switzerland, Wales and Montenegro.

Gareth Barry

Born: Hastings; February 23, 1981

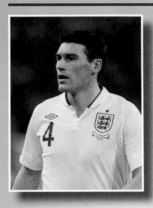

Gareth Barry will be delighted to have become a regular in an England shirt after a four-year period of international football exile under Sven-Goran Eriksson.

The Manchester City midfielder has largely reinvented himself, having become established at former club Aston Villa as a defender. He made his senior England debut – against Ukraine in 2000 at the age of 19 – as a left back and made 27 appearances for England's Under-21s.

But Barry, who has captained England on several occasions, became a lynchpin of Martin O'Neil's midfield at Villa Park, and attracted interest from Liverpool before moving to Manchester City in 2009, where he has since won the Premier League and FA Cup.

During his latter days in Birmingham and since his move to City, Barry established himself as an England regular under Fabio Capello, after Steve McClaren initially recalled him to the set-up in 2007. He missed Euro 2012 through injury but played in three of England's four games at the 2010 World Cup in South Africa.

MIDFIELDERS

Frank Lampard
Born: Romford, London; June 20, 1978

Frank Lampard laid a major ghost to rest when he helped Chelsea win last year's Champions League, even scoring a penalty in the shoot-out in the Final.

A superb goalscoring midfielder, Lampard has excelled for both Chelsea and England, for whom he is the all-time leading scorer of penalties. He is approaching 100 international caps and has won three Premier League titles, four FA Cups and two League Cups with the west London club

In May 2012, Chelsea beat Bayern Munich on penalties – with Lampard captaining the side on the night – to win the Champions League for the first time -- a just reward for Lampard after he was forced to endure three semi-final exits and a painful penalty shoot-out loss to Manchester United in the Moscow Final of 2008 before finally getting his hands on club football's greatest prize.

The east London-born player, who has captained England as well as Chelsea, began his career at his father's old club, West Ham United. He started his senior international career while with the Hammers, winning his first cap in a 1999 friendly win over Belgium.

Despite injury depriving him of a role at Euro 2012, Lampard has appeared in three major tournaments and was named in UEFA's Team of the Tournament at Euro 2004. Luck seems to have deserted him at World Cups; he missed a penalty in the 2006 quarter-final defeat to Portugal and was denied a goal against Germany in the last 16 in 2010 when the officials wrongly judged his shot to have not crossed the line.

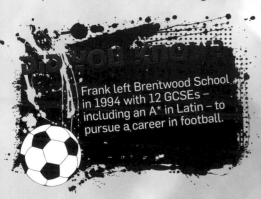
Frank left Brentwood School in 1994 with 12 GCSEs – including an A* in Latin – to pursue a career in football.

James Milner
Born: Leeds; January 4, 1986

Roy Hodgson made James Milner a starter in each one of his teams at Euro 2012 and the Manchester City midfielder will be hoping to remain a regular for the national side if his total of senior caps is to get close to the record 46 appearances he made for the Under-21s.

The Yorkshire-born player began his career at his hometown club, having been a ball boy and season ticket holder at Leeds United's Elland Road ground before joining them as a player at the age of 10.

His time at Leeds was cut short by the club's financial struggles and in 2004 they were forced to sell Milner to Newcastle, where he spent a mixed four years falling in and out of favour, before joining Aston Villa in 2008 having enjoyed a period on loan in Birmingham two years previously.

A tough, no-nonsense player, typically seen wearing short sleeves in sub-zero temperatures, Milner has a deceptive turn of pace and has proved equally adept on the wing as in central midfield. He flourished at Villa under the tutelage of Martin O'Neill, his dynamic performances earning him a senior England debut in 2009 and a place in the 2010 World Cup squad.

His 2010 transfer to Manchester City has brought him Premier League and FA Cup winners' medals and he has now become a regular fixture in the national side.

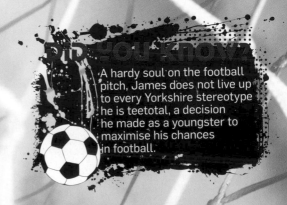
A hardy soul on the football pitch, James does not live up to every Yorkshire stereotype – he is teetotal, a decision he made as a youngster to maximise his chances in football.

Theo Walcott
Born: Stanmore, London; March 16, 1989

The blisteringly quick Theo Walcott showed by the way he transformed England's match with Sweden at Euro 2012 – and in the process, arguably, their tournament – how important he could be to his country in years to come.

Although now usually employed on the right side of midfield, Walcott emerged as a supremely talented striker at Southampton. After making his senior debut aged only 16 and appearing only 21 more times for the Saints after that, Arsenal were so convinced of his worth that they paid nearly £12million for him in 2006.

After being gradually converted to a winger at Arsenal, Walcott's progress has not always been smooth – injuries and Arsene Wenger's desire to progress him gently have periodically limited his first team appearances – but he has now played in over 200 matches for the north London club.

Walcott became England's youngest ever player – 17 years and 75 days – after making a substitute appearance in a friendly against Hungary in May 2006 and was controversially selected for Sven-Goran Eriksson's 2006 World Cup squad even though he had yet to make a senior appearance for Arsenal.

Having played 21 times for the Under-21s, Walcott scored a hat-trick for the senior team against Croatia in September 2008 on only his second start. The Londoner was surprisingly omitted from the 2010 World Cup squad but his impact at Euro 2012 suggests he has a long international career ahead.

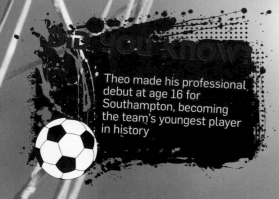

Theo made his professional debut at age 16 for Southampton, becoming the team's youngest player in history

Jordan Henderson
Born: Sunderland; June 17, 1990

Jordan Henderson could be said to have risen from obscurity to a major tournament in the blink of an eye with the upturn in fortunes enjoyed by the Liverpool player.

When England were in South Africa for the 2010 World Cup, Henderson was merely a highly rated prospect, still in the infancy of his career at Sunderland.

Twelve months on, after playing in all but one of Sunderland's Premier League matches in the 2010-11 season en route to winning the club's Young Player of the Year award for the second year running, Henderson so impressed Kenny Dalglish that the then-Liverpool manager decided to offer Sunderland £16 for his services, which was an sum the Wearside club could not refuse.

Henderson made his senior England debut while still playing for his hometown club, starting in a friendly against France in November 2010. The midfielder also represented the Under-21s at the 2011 European Championship and capped an incredible rise to the top with his inclusion in Roy Hodgson's squad for Euro 2012, making substitute appearances at the tournament against France and Italy.

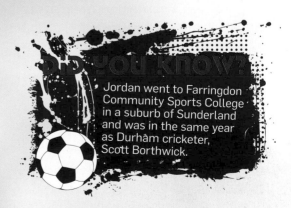

Jordan went to Farringdon Community Sports College in a suburb of Sunderland and was in the same year as Durham cricketer, Scott Borthwick.

Alex Oxlade-Chamberlain

Born: Portsmouth; August 15, 1993

Alex Oxlade-Chamberlain marked the end of a dramatic first season in the Premier League at Arsenal by appearing for England at Euro 2012, starting his country's opening match with France. It followed a debut for the senior team -- after four goals in eight appearances for the Under-21s - in a warm-up match for Euro 2012 in May.

The 19-year-old cost Arsenal a fee that, with prospective add-ons, could eventually total £15m when they bought him in 2011. Such a large investment from Arsène Wenger immediately seemed justified as the young man shone in an Arsenal team that at the time was struggling for confidence.

His debut for the Gunners came in a disastrous 8-2 defeat at Manchester United but the Ox, as he has become known at the Emirates, soon scored his first goals for the club and became Arsenal's youngest ever Champions League goalscorer after netting against Olympiakos.

Wenger, who famously refused to rush Theo Walcott's development as a youngster, had few such worries about Oxlade-Chamberlain, handing him his first start against Manchester United in January last year. A month later he received widespread praise for his energetic performance against AC Milan in the Champions League.

Oxlade-Chamberlain began his career at Southampton, as an academy graduate, and helped the Saints win promotion from League One to the Championship in 2011.

Although his father, Mark, played football for England, Alex attended a school that played only cricket and rugby and was offered a trial by rugby team London Irish.

Scott Parker

Born: Kennington, London; October 13, 1980.

Now 32, Scott Parker has had to be patient in his wait to be an England regular. In the late stages of Fabio Capello's time in charge, however, that finally became a reality.

Londoner Parker has always attracted praise for his precocious talent in central midfield, especially his ability to read a game and control its tempo. He impressed at Charlton Athletic, where he made 145 first team appearances, before becoming one of Roman Abramovich's first buys at Chelsea.

He failed to force his way into the first team regularly in west London and went to Newcastle in 2005 for what have so far been the only two years of his career spent outside of London.

The Tottenham midfielder returned to the capital in 2007 to play for West Ham, where his committed, no-nonsense football quickly made him a fans' favourite. When the Hammers were relegated to the Championship in 2011, he crossed the city to join Spurs.

Parker's senior international career has been a stop-start one. He made his debut in 2003 and went five years without winning a cap until becoming a regular in 2011. He captained his country against Holland in the February of the following year when Stuart Pearce was in temporary charge and featured in his first major tournament at the age of 31 at Euro 2012.

When Scott replaced Frank Lampard in a friendly against Denmark in 2011, he became the first England player to win his first four caps while playing for four different clubs.

ST. GEORGE'S PARK

Establishing a National Football Centre in England moved from dream to reality when St. George's Park opened in 2012.

The £100 million complex – on a 330-acre site in Burton upon Trent in Staffordshire – was more than a decade in the making and an aspiration for many years before that.

There was a drive to set the development in motion towards the late 1990s and the land was acquired by The Football Association in 2001 but various business plans proved unviable and progress stalled.

But after England failed to qualify for Euro 2008 it was reignited under the leadership of David Sheepshanks, whose vision was to create a National Football Centre to rival the internationally-renowned facilities at Clairefontaine in France and Coverciano in Italy, as well as world champions Spain's Ciudad de Football. The end result is an even bigger, better and more far-reaching development than originally envisaged.

The main function of St. George's Park is to be a world-class training facility, with the focus on coach education and cutting-edge sports science and medicine, as well as providing a training home for the 24 England teams to rival any in the world.

The centre was named St. George's Park to honour England's patron saint and to inspire national pride and unity.

But it will not be a facility for the exclusive use of England's international teams. It will also be the centre of the game right down to the grassroots, accessible to everyone, with organisations from every level represented.

It will become an educational hub to help reinforce coaching as a recognised profession, with qualification pathways and career opportunities, and provide the first FIFA Centre of Medical Excellence in England, open to everyone.

And with a superb hotel and conference facilities, it will also be a place where sport and business can interact.

The FA has been grateful for the help of several like-minded commercial partners in bringing the project to fruition, with substantial backing from Umbro, the renowned football brand and long-term FA partner, and support from Hilton Worldwide, the world-famous hotelier.

"When we didn't qualify for the Euros in 2008 that was the starting point and then we had another sharp reminder in our disappointment at the 2010 World Cup Finals in South Africa," Sheepshanks said.

"We had two big wake-up calls at two big tournaments in succession and now we have had another – not just England but other countries – from what Spain have taught us.

"Their performance in Kiev (in winning Euro 2012) confirmed the decisions taken to build St. George's Park were absolutely the right ones.

"Hopefully the rest of the world will see this as a statement of intent by English football, which we will go on seeking to improve."

ROAD TO RIO

Spotlight on England's opponents in Qualifying Group H

Poland

HEAD TO HEAD
England   9 wins
Poland   1 wins
Draws 5

Tuesday, October 16, 2012
POLAND V ENGLAND

Tuesday, October 15, 2013
ENGLAND V POLAND

After hosting Euro 2012 alongside Ukraine, Poland will be hoping to reach their third World Cup Finals in the last four in Brazil in 2014.

After 16 years without a major tournament appearance, the Poles qualified for the 2002 World Cup in Japan and South Korea, going out at the group stage. They qualified again four years later despite being beaten twice by England – the last occasions the nations met – but their stay at the Finals in Germany was similarly brief.

England and Poland are familiar World Cup rivals, having been grouped together in five qualification campaigns. The first, in 1973, remains the most famous, less so for Poland's only competitive victory against England – 2-0 in Chorzow in June of that year – than for their performance at Wembley in the October return. Thanks to an outstanding display by goalkeeper Jan Tomaszewski, the Poles held England to a 1-1 draw to qualify for the 1974 Finals at England's expense and went on to claim third place in the tournament.

This marked the beginning of Poland's golden era, characterised by their greatest ever player, Zibi Boniek. The former Juventus and Roma star led Poland to the semi-finals of the 1982 World Cup, where they were beaten by eventual champions Italy, before beating France 3-2 in a pulsating 3rd place play-off match, arguably Poland's greatest ever performance.

Poland had a disappointing Euro 2008 and failed even to qualify for the last World Cup. They showed flashes of quality at Euro 2012 and England will be especially wary of their Borussia Dortmund trio, Robert Lewandowski, Lukasz Piszczek and Polish captain Jakub Blaszczykowski.

The England team in history – 40 years ago

All good things must come to an end; and so it was with the reign of Sir Alf Ramsey. Although it was not until 1974 that The FA decided his time was over, the parting of the ways seemed inevitable after the extraordinary performance of a Polish goalkeeper at Wembley on October 17, 1973.

Ramsey had won one World Cup and reached the quarter-finals of another but in a three-team qualifying group for the 1974 Finals there was no room for error. England's failure to beat Wales at home after winning 1-0 in Cardiff was compounded when they lost 2-0 to Poland in Chorzow.

This left them needing to defeat Poland at home in the final match. For the Poles a draw would be enough to take them through and they were aided by an astonishing display by goalkeeper Jan Tomaszewski.

England had 35 attempts on goal to Poland's two and hit the woodwork several times but Tomaszewski - famously dubbed a 'clown' by Brian Clough in his role as TV pundit - was beaten only from the penalty spot, saving everything else with hands, feet, legs, fists, fingertips and any part of his frame he could get in the way.

To make things more difficult for England, an error by defender Norman Hunter had allowed Poland to take a 55th-minute lead, which meant that though Allan Clarke did manage to get the ball past The Clown from the spot eight minutes later, it was not enough.

With 1966 World Cup winning captain Bobby Moore playing his 108th and last match for England against Italy in November, 1973 really was the end of an era.

POLAND - TEAM 1-TOMASZEWSKi
2-SZYMANOWSKI 3-GORGON
4-MUSIAL 5-BULZACKI 6-KASP-
ERCZAK 7-LATO 8-CMIKIEWICZ
9-DEYNA 10-DOMARSKI 11-GADOCHA

STRIKERS

Andy Carroll

Born: Gateshead
January 6, 1989

The most expensive British player of all time has not been without critics since moving to Liverpool in 2011, but Andy Carroll has begun to produce performances for both Liverpool and England that have gone some way to justifying his £35m price tag.

The Tyneside-born striker had made only 33 Premier League appearances for his hometown club before moving to Anfield, although he did score 17 Championship goals in 2010 to help fire Newcastle United back to the top flight after their relegation the previous year.

At first Liverpool's style of play seemed ill-suited to Carroll's strengths as he struggled for goals but, in the latter half of the 2011-12 season, he seemed to find his feet at Anfield, helping the club win the Carling Cup before he scored the winning goal against Everton in an FA Cup Semi-Final at Wembley.

Immensely strong and very tall, Carroll has the attributes to be a top quality centre-forward. His heading prowess was perfectly illustrated by the goal that gave England first blood against Sweden at Euro 2012; he cleverly drifted into space in the box, leapt high above all around him and powered the ball into the net with his distinctive pony-tail flapping behind him.

After appearing for his country at Under-19 and Under-21 levels, Carroll made his debut for the senior team against France in November 2010 and was an integral member of Roy Hodgson's 23-man squad at Euro 2012.

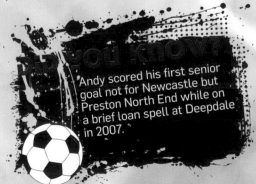

DID YOU KNOW? Andy scored his first senior goal not for Newcastle but Preston North End while on a brief loan spell at Deepdale in 2007.

Darren Bent

Born: Tooting, London
February 6, 1984

Darren Bent remains one of the Premier League's most potent English goalscorers despite a disappointing year with Aston Villa and was unfortunate to miss Euro 2012 through injury.

The Londoner first impressed at Ipswich Town in the Championship, scoring 54 goals in three seasons for the Tractor Boys. He moved to Premier League Charlton Athletic in 2005 and was the highest scoring Englishman in the 2005-06 Premier League season, winning the Addicks' Player of the Season award.

When Charlton were relegated in 2007, Bent was not short of suitors and ended up moving to Tottenham although his progress at White Hart Lane was halted by fierce competition for places.

Bent moved on again in 2009, this time opting for the north-east in Sunderland, where a season-and-a-half of prolific goalscoring persuaded Aston Villa to pay a club record fee of £24m for Bent in January 2010.

A player with a deadly finish and intelligent movement, Bent made his debut for England against Uruguay in 2006, but has only recently become a regular. He missed the Euro 2012 Finals but scored three crucial goals in qualifying, against Switzerland, Wales and Montenegro, the first of those his maiden international goal.

DID YOU KNOW? Darren once got a mention on top soap Coronation Street. His name was dropped into a conversation about fantasy football. Not bad for a soap that normally focuses on the fictitious 'Weatherfield Town'.

Wayne Rooney

Born: Liverpool
October 24, 1985

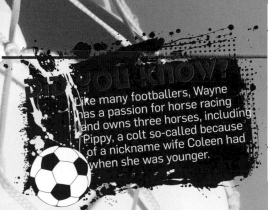

The powerful forward came through Everton's youth system and made his senior debut at Goodison Park when only 16 years old. He became the youngest scorer in the history of the Premier League when he netted against Arsenal on Octoner 19, 2002 – five days before his 17th birthday

One of England's most recognisable sportsmen, Manchester United's Wayne Rooney was unable to inspire his country to glory at Euro 2012 on returning from suspension but remains a key component of the national side.

The Liverpudlian has every club honour except for The FA Cup at Old Trafford, including four Premier League titles and a Champions League winners' medal. Having reached 75 senior England caps by the age of 26, appearing in four major tournaments along the way, it would be a surprise if Rooney does not go on to top 100 appearances for the national side.

Always seemingly destined for stardom, Rooney left Goodison Park for Old Trafford in 2004, United manager Sir Alex Ferguson paying £25.6m for his services. The tone for his time at United was immediately set when Rooney scored a hat-trick on his Champions League debut against Fenerbahce. He scored his 100th United goal against Wigan in 2009.

Rooney rose to stardom so fast he skipped England's Under- 21s and became England's youngest ever senior player when he appeared against Australia in February 2003, aged just 17 years and 111 days.

Jermain Defoe

Born: Beckton, London
October 7, 1982

Jermain Defoe has been one of the Premier League's deadliest finishers, a quality he has also shown on the international stage.

The striker came to prominence first during a loan spell at Bournemouth in 2000-01, where he scored 18 goals in 29 League games, a spell that included scoring in ten consecutive matches.

He became a favourite at then-parent club West Ham on returning to Upton Park, displaying his natural instincts as a goal poacher by scoring 41 times for the east London club. Six months after the club's relegation from the Premier League, however, Defoe was tempted into a move to Tottenham.

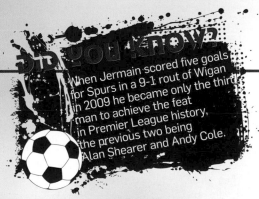

Under manager Martin Jol, Defoe at first shone at White Hart Lane but eventually fell out of favour and he linked up again with ex-West Ham boss Harry Redknapp at Portsmouth, before following Redknapp back to Tottenham soon afterwards.

Defoe has been to two World Cups with England, and scored the goal against Slovenia that took England into the last 16 at the 2010 Finals. The same year, he scored a hat-trick in a Euro 2012 qualifier against Bulgaria at Wembley and went to the Finals in Poland and Ukraine as a member of Roy Hodgson's 23-man squad.

STRIKERS

Danny Welbeck

Born: Manchester; November 26, 1990.

Danny Welbeck produced some impressive performances at Euro 2012 and is tipped to forge a long career in international football.

The Manchester United man has scored goals at five different levels for England, starting with the Under-17s in 2006. His winning goal against Belgium at Wembley in June last year was his maiden international strike and he followed it with some superb displays at the Euros, notably scoring the decisive goal in the 3-2 win against Sweden.

The Mancunian made his debut for his hometown club in 2008 but it was during a season-long loan at Sunderland in 2010-11 that he underlined his potential, scoring his first goal of six for the Wearsiders in a memorable 3-0 win at Chelsea.

He returned to Old Trafford for the 2011-12 season and became an established regular in the first team, scoring 12 goals in 40 appearances.

Regularly paired with Wayne Rooney for both United and England, Welbeck is more than just a goalscorer. He is adept at holding the ball up and bringing his strike partner or midfield team-mates into play. He also proved effective as a lone striker for England at Euro 2012.

Daniel Sturridge

Born: Birmingham; September 1, 1989.

Chelsea's Daniel Sturridge could consider himself unfortunate after narrowly missing out on a place in Roy Hodgson's 23-man squad for Euro 2012 but the winger-cum-forward still looks to have the promise of a long international career ahead of him.

Sturridge started out at Manchester City and was highly thought of at Eastlands, winning the club's Young Player of the Year award in 2008-09. Yet he was allowed to leave City for Chelsea in July 2009.

He appeared only periodically for Chelsea in his first 18 months at Stamford Bridge before his potential became obvious during a loan spell with Bolton Wanderers in 2010-11 that brought him eight goals in 12 matches, form that prompted new Chelsea manager Andre Villas-Boas to make Sturridge part of his plans.

A highly promising 2011-12 season saw Sturridge help the Blues to FA Cup and Champions League glory, scoring 13 goals along the way. His performances also gained him senior international recognition for the first time, his debut coming against Sweden at Wembley in November 2011. He was also named in Stuart Pearce's 18-man Team GB squad for the London 2012 Olympics.

ROAD TO RIO

Spotlight on England's opponents in Qualifying Group H

Montenegro

HEAD TO HEAD
England   0 wins
Montenegro 0 wins
Draws 2

Tuesday, March 26, 2013
MONTENEGRO V ENGLAND

Friday, October 11, 2013
ENGLAND V MONTENEGRO

England will be confronting familiar foes in Montenegro when they play the former Yugoslav state twice in 2013. The recently independent country – formerly part of Serbia & Montenegro – drew twice with England in qualification for Euro 2012 to secure an unlikely play-off place.

Home to only 625,000 people, little more than one percent of England's population, the minnows held England to a goalless Wembley draw before coming back from 2-0 down to draw 2-2 in Podgorica in 2011.

Despite the country's modest size, the talent of some of Montenegro's players should not be underestimated and many ply their trade with Europe's top clubs. Stefan Savic is an emerging talent at Manchester City, captain Mirko Vucinic plays for Juventus, defender Marko Basa is employed by French club Lille and Fiorentina's young forward Stevan Jovetic is one of Europe's most highly sought-after players.

Montenegro did not play a full international fixture until 2007 – a 2-1 win over Hungary – but already harbour aspirations of being the smallest nation by population ever to qualify for a World Cup. England will want to ensure they are not the ones who miss out for the eastern European nation to break that record.

Bobby Robson's time as England manager was one of highs and lows. The highs were his two World Cups, the lows his European Championships. England failed to qualify for his first, in 1984, but did so in style four years later, conceding only one goal in six qualification matches, which they wrapped up with a stunning 4-1 victory over Yugoslavia in Belgrade that established them as favourites to challenge hosts West Germany.

Yet the Finals themselves went disastrously wrong. For the first time in England's history, they returned home from a major tournament without winning a single point.

But while losing 1-0 to Republic of Ireland was an embarrassment, when England were trounced by Holland in Dusseldorf they simply came up against an exceptional team, built around the magical qualities of Ruud Gullit, Frank Rijkaard and Marco van Basten.

The England line-up did not lack talent, combining the skills of Gary Lineker, Peter Beardsley, John Barnes and Glenn Hoddle with the industry of Bryan Robson and the resilience of Tony Adams. They were simply torn apart.

Van Basten put Holland ahead in the first half, Bryan Robson equalised early in the second. But with Gullit pulling the strings the Dutch found another gear and two goals in four minutes completed a devastating hat-trick for Van Basten, with no one more disappointed than Peter Shilton, who was making his 100th appearance as England goalkeeper.

Holland went on to win the tournament, Van Basten lighting up the Final with one of the goals of the century - a perfect far-post volley from a seemingly impossible angle - in a 2-0 win over the Soviet Union.

ENGLAND WOMEN

England's women on the up

The England women's team have become regular contenders at the business end of major tournaments under head coach Hope Powell, reaching the quarter-finals of the 2007 and 2011 World Cups and finishing runners-up to Germany in the UEFA European Women's Championship after reaching the 2009 Final in Finland.

Rachel Brown

Their success has attracted more girls to take up the game in England and raised the profile of stars such as goalkeeper Rachel Brown, midfielder Fara Williams and striker Rachel Yankey.

The focus for 2013 is the European Championship in Sweden, which begin on July 10 and finish with the Final in Solna on July 28. Germany, the dominant force in the women's game, are bidding to win a sixth consecutive title.

Rachel Yankey

Fara Williams

England v Iceland, Rachel Brown saves a penalty during the penalty shoot-out

Ellen White
Player of the Year as voted for by fans

Wordsearch

Hidden in the grid are the surnames of 18 players who have captained England. Can you find them all? Answers on p61.

Find the words in the grid. Words can go horizontally, vertically and diagonally in all eight directions.

W	L	C	R	M	G	R	F	Q	D	R	Z	P	N	Z
L	R	J	M	O	Q	L	C	P	P	M	E	N	S	X
N	E	I	R	L	B	K	K	R	R	A	N	S	H	Q
F	F	R	G	S	L	S	L	P	R	M	M	Z	E	B
N	T	H	O	H	E	V	O	C	L	A	C	L	A	T
W	T	M	D	O	T	H	E	N	D	D	T	V	R	J
I	A	Z	M	J	M	C	G	A	M	R	K	M	E	C
L	L	T	H	E	K	W	B	U	K	A	K	Y	R	P
K	P	K	C	E	B	M	J	H	H	R	W	R	Q	M
I	G	N	E	T	E	R	R	Y	C	R	Y	E	A	P
N	I	G	R	E	K	E	N	I	L	E	K	H	X	Y
S	A	L	X	V	W	H	N	R	Z	G	K	C	B	M
N	M	L	C	W	K	W	L	F	D	C	R	T	Z	Q
S	H	I	L	T	O	N	P	N	E	W	O	U	B	C
K	L	V	T	N	K	Z	Y	B	W	C	W	B	K	P

Adams	**Keegan**	**Robson**
Beckham	**Lineker**	**Shearer**
Butcher	**Moore**	**Shilton**
Gerrard	**Owen**	**Terry**
Hughes	**Pearce**	**Wilkins**
Ince	**Platt**	**Wright**

Spotlight

on the England Under-21s

The England Under-21's are the last rung on the age-group ladder in the England international structure and the feeder team for the senior squad.

Established stars such as Frank Lampard, James Milner and Gareth Barry played for the Under-21s before graduating to the full international set-up. Milner holds the record for most Under-21 caps after making his debut as an 18-year-old and clocking up 46 appearances.

Current Under-21 squad members include Birmingham goalkeeper Jack Butland, Tottenham defender Steven Caulker, Chelsea midfielder Josh McEachran and Sunderland forward Connor Wickham.

England won the European Under-21 Championship twice in the 1980s and were losing Finalists in 2009, when they were beaten by Germany.

Several members of the current squad were members of Team GB at the 2012 London Olympics, with Under-21 manager Stuart Pearce at the helm.

The focus for 2013 will be the European Championship Finals in Israel from June 15 to 28.

Connor Wickham

The Sunderland striker made his Football League debut with Ipswich aged just 16 years and 11 days and scored the winning goal in the UEFA European Under-17 Championship Final.

Steven Caulker

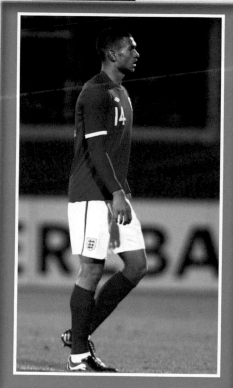

London-born centre back Steven is a product of the Tottenham Hotspur Academy who made his name in the Premier League with a season-long loan to Swansea City, helping the newly-promoted Welsh side enjoy a successful first season in the top flight.

Josh McEachran

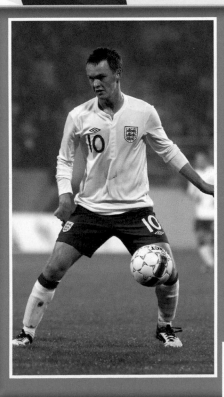

Midfielder Josh has Champions League and Premier League experience with Chelsea and Swansea. He captained England's Under-17s and made his Under-21 debut while still eligible for that age group in November 2010.

The England team in history - 20 years ago

Losing to a United States team made up of part-time players at the 1950 World Cup Finals may be top of the list of the England team's most embarrassing moments, but the goal they conceded to San Marino in 1993 comes in a close second.

It came as Graham Taylor's team clung to the hope that a shock result in Poznan and a hatful of goals in Bologna might somehow spare them the indignity of failing to qualify for the 1994 World Cup Finals.

England's chance had all but gone anyway, with defeat to Holland in Rotterdam in October. The result rankled with Taylor after Ronald Koeman escaped a red card for a cynical 'professional' foul on England's David Platt and, having stayed on the pitch, put Holland ahead in an even game from a twice-taken free kick. The Dutch went on to win 2-0.

It meant England would be going to the United States the following summer only if they beat San Marino by seven clear goals in their final game in November, and Holland lost to Poland the same evening.

In the event, Holland's 3-1 win in Poznan made it all academic, but England's calamitous start to their game, played in Bologna, only made their faces redder. An under-hit back-pass by Stuart Pearce allowed the minnows to score after only eight seconds - the fastest goal in World Cup history, and from a side that had scored only once in their whole qualifying campaign up to that moment.

England recovered to win 7-1, although even that comprehensive margin was one short of what they had needed. Taylor resigned within days, clearing the way for Terry Venables to take charge.

QUIZ ANSWERS

1. Gary Lineker, against Poland in 1986.
2. Sir Bobby Robson, between 1982-1990.
3. David Beckham and Wayne Rooney.
4. France and Germany (both 28 times).
5. Steven Gerrard, who was selected for the 2002 Finals but had to withdraw through injury.
6. Three times, at the 1968 European Championship, the 1990 World Cup in Italy and at Euro '96.
7. 14 (Old Trafford, City of Manchester Stadium, Elland Road, White Hart Lane, Upton Park, Anfield, Portman Road, Walkers Stadium, Pride Park, Villa Park, Stadium of Light, Riverside Stadium, St Mary's Stadium and St James' Park).
8. Gary Lineker.
9. Paul Scholes with 14 to Gazza's 10.
10. Ukraine, in May 2000.
11. Switzerland and Finland.
12. Bryan Robson, who scored after 27 seconds against France in the 1982 World Cup Finals and after 38 seconds of a friendly against Yugoslavia at Wembley in 1989.
13. Tony Adams, who scored the second goal in a 2-0 win over Ukraine in 2000.
14. Liverpool, with six.
15. Ashley Young, by 107 days.
16. The 1994 World Cup in the United States.
17. Steven Gerrard, who gave England the lead after four minutes against the United States.
18. None. The Southampton star failed to find the net in eight senior appearances.
19. Kevin Keegan, with four from 18 games in charge. Hoddle lost five from 28.
20. In 1999, in a Euro 2000 play-off second leg at Wembley.

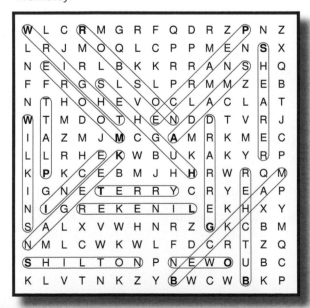